NIMROD

A Three-Act Play

To watch the play, please scan the following QR Code:
NIMROD

Dr. Sultan bin Muhammad Al-Qasimi

NIMROD

A Three-Act Play

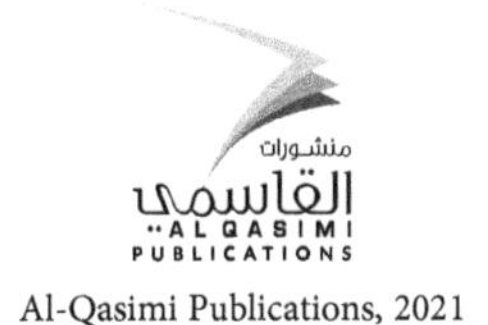

Al-Qasimi Publications, 2021

Book Title: NIMROD (A Three-Act Play)
First published in 2008 in Arabic as "Al-Namrud" by : Al-Qasimi Publications
Author: Dr. Sultan bin Muhammad Al-Qasimi (United Arab Emirates)
Publisher Name: Al-Qasimi Publications
Sharjah, United Arab Emirates
Edition: Second
Year of publication: 2021

ISBN: 978-9948-36-056-8
Printing Permission: National Media Council, Abu Dhabi, UAE
No. MC 01-03-4836518, Date: 17-07-2019

Age Classification: E
The age group that matches the content of the books was classified according to the age classification issued by the National Council for Media
----
Al- Qasimi Publications, Al Tarfa, Sheikh Mohammed Bin Zayed Road
PO Box 64009 Sharjah, United Arab Emirates
Tel: 0097165090000, Fax: 0097165520070
Email: info@aqp.ae

Cover picture: Babel by: Pieter Bruegel,
Künst historisches Museum, Vienna, Austria

CONTENTS

Introduction **7**

Al-Nimrod (Nimrod) **9**

Play characters **13**

Act 1 **15**

Scene 1 17

Scene 2 21

Act 2 **25**

Scene 1 27

Scene 2 32

Scene 3 35

Act 3 **37**

Scene 1 39

Scene 2 43

Introduction

Al-Nimrod (Nimrod)

Prophet Ibrahim and Nimrod

I was asked about prophet Ibahim's relation to Nimrod.

Herein a clarification:

In reference of the ancient historical book of Torah and the New Testament, the following has become apparent:

Firstly:

Consulting the book of 'Genesis' particularly in the period of history within the New Testament, chapter 10 mentions that the prophet Noah, peace be upon him, had two sons named Sam and Ham.

One of Ham's sons is named Canaan, he is the

father of Nimrod, however Ham's other son Kosh is said to also be one of Nimrod's brothers known as the Hamites. Chapter 11 of the Genesis book mentions that the prophet Ibrahim is of the descendants of Shem, the Semites, and they come in the following respect:

1. Arphaxad, son of Shem
2. Shelah, son of Arphaxad
3. Eber, son of Shelah
4. Peleg, son of Eber
5. Reu, son of Peleg
6. Serug, son of Reu
7. Nahor, son of Serug
8. Terah, son of Nahor
9. Abram (Abraham), son of Terah

What is listed above has been identically mentioned in the Torah.

Secondly:

The Book of Jubliess, written in the first century before Christ and is highly respected by the Jews, deliberates on the history of the Jews and mentions that Nimrod is the father of Azurad, wife of Eber, son of Shelah and the mother of Peleg. Herein, the book considers prophet Ibrahim to be a seventh-generation descendant of Nimrod.

Thirdly:

The Book of Rolls, a manuscript found in Sinai dating back to the first century after Christ, states that Nimrod had lived in a different time period from that of Ibrahim's.

Based on this information we find that Nimrod had lived in the same timeframe as Shelah, as Nimrod's daughter married to the son of Shelah.

The question remains as to where prophet Ibrahim and Nimrod are mentioned in conjunction?

Consulting the book of Heggada written by a group of Jews in the third century, prophet Ibrahim is mentioned to have met with Nimrod, however this source fails to reference historical content from the Torah and the Bible.

Muslim historians state the following in their books:

1. In Ibn Kathir's book Early Days, historian Emad Eddin Abol Fidaa Ismail bin Amr bin Kathir discusses the debate around prophet Ibrahim's presence with Nimrod. His view is based on interpreters alluding to this encounter, and he mentions how Qatada ibn Di'ama, Ismail ibn Abd al-Rahman Suddi and Mohamed bin Ishak refer to this debate to have taken place between prophet Ibrahim and Nimrod.
2. In The Complete History book, the author

EzzEddin Abol Hassan bin AbilKaram al-Shaibani, known as Ali ibn al-Athir, states that his information regarding the debate between prophet Ibrahim and Nimrod is derived from Zaid ibn Aslam, then said: "he mentioned a group of anonymous people" and named some unknown to them.

3. Muhammad ibn Jarir al-Tabari mentions the debate in his book History of the Prophets and Kings.
4. The debate is also discussed in the book General History by Abu Hanifa Ahmad ibn Dawoud Dinawari.
5. The debate is similarly discussed in the book "Kanz AlDurar wa Jami AlGhurar" by Abo Bakr Abdullah bin Aibak al-Dowadari.

All that is mentioned above are unreliable sayings that cannot be counted on.

Dr. Sultan bin Muhammad Al Qasimi

Play characters

(According to their appearance)

- The announcer
- A group of people
- The person
- King Dahhak
- King Dahhak's entourage
- Another person
- A Third person
- A Fourth person
- The man (Kapi the blacksmith)
- A revered man – Shelah bin Arphaxad
- Companions of Shelah
- A group of men
- One of them
- Nimrod

- Heavily armed soldiers
- The crowd
- First person in the crowd
- Second person in the crowd
- Third person in the crowd
- The ministers
- Nimrod's entourage
- The minister
- Applicants (from the crowd)
- First applicant
- Second applicant
- Third applicant
- Treasury official
- Construction Expert
- Everyone
- The gathered public
- Some of the workers
- The angel
- The army commander
- The first soldier
- The second soldier
- Group of citizens (A)
- One of the group of citizens (A)
- Group of citizens (B)
- One of the group of citizens (B)

Act 1

Scene 1

Before the curtains are raised..

The announcer: The place.. The land of Babel.

The time period.. Four thousand years ago.

The scenery:

The curtains rise showing a scenery.. To the right appears a mountain with a cave, and on the other side along with the backdrop, trees are showing.

A group of people are sitting on one side of the stage.

A person enters from the left side of the stage, yelling at people, while the stage is to the right side.

The Person: Byorasb, King Dahhak is coming.. King Dahhak! Run away.. Run!

All the people on the stage fall to the ground in fear and horror.

King Dahhak enters the stage from the backside. Two bulges in the shape of a serpent's head sit on his shoulders, and he covers them with a cape.

Whenever he encounters people he would uncover the bulges, shake his body and project intimidating shouts, so as to cause the serpents heads to move and appear real to people.. His entourage then follows him as he gets off stage.

One of the persons on the floor of the stage then jumps up to the center of the stage and says in amazement:

The Person: have you seen the two serpents on his shoulders, Oh my kind God!.. Oh my kind God, they are frightening.

Another person: They are not real.. He wants to scare people.. week-minded people like you.

Third person: When he dominated the nation, evil and immorality appeared through him.

Fourth person: He dominated the whole world filling it with injustice and oppression and killed people.

A man called Kapi enters the stage holding a thick stick raising at its tip a leather sheet, as he is a blacksmith he would use it to protect himself from fire.
Dahhak had murdered two of his sons.. He started wailing and saying:

Kapi: He killed my sons.. He killed my sons!

Fourth person *(addressing the third person)*: you heard that? It is Kapi the blacksmith, from Isfahan, Dahhak killed two of his sons.. He goes across the nations pleading to revolt against Dahhak.

Third person *(calling upon Kapi):* Kapi!.. Come here.

Kapi does not turn to him, he continues his call and moves around the stage saying:

Kapi: Revolt against Dahhak before he kills you!

The Fourth person *calling upon him:* Kapi..

Kapi *(continues his call):* Revolt against Dahhak before he kills you!

The Fourth person (*calling upon him)*: Kapi..

Kapi *(continues his call)*: Revolt against Dahhak before he kills you!

The Fourth person grabs Kapi from the shoulders, as if he was waking him up, saying:

Fourth person: If we revolt, who is going to be our king? You Kapi?

Kapi: I am one of the public, I am not qualified to be a king.

Fourth person: Who then?

Kapi: The king should be of royal blood.

At this point, a highly revered man with his companions enter.

Third person: This is the son of kings, Shelah bin Arphaxad.

Fourth person: Move forward Shelah, son of the kings and to be the king of Babel.

Shelah: I do not have the power to fight Dahhak, but let us send a message to Nimrod bin Kanaan, he is a mighty man who could help us against Dahhak.

Everybody: Agreed..

Shelah: Let us go to Nimrod.

Everybody: To Nimrod.. To Nimrod.

Blackout

Scene 2

The stage lights turn on, a group of men stand looking to one side of the stage, one of them yells out:

One of them: He has arrived.. He has arrived.. Nimrod has arrived!

A huge man swaggering triumphantly enters and heavily armed soldiers stand behind him:

Nimrod: I have arrested everyone from the house of Dahhak who happened to be in Babel. I struck them very hard until they were all dead under the lashes of my whip.. Where is Dahhak? He ran away! He disappeared! Come out and face me Dahhak! You coward!

Dahhak enters the stage with his former dress:

Dahhak: You call me coward when you are a killer of women and children?

Dahhak charges at Nimrod with a spear, but Nimrod evades the spear with his whip and hits Dahhak with an iron rod which took him down, Nimrod then presses his foot onto Dahhak's neck and orders his soldiers to tighten his handcuffs:

Nimrod: Soldiers, tighten his handcuffs and bring him before me.

Having tightened his handcuffs, the soldiers bring Dahhak before Nimrod.

Nimrod takes off the snake-headed bulges on Dahhak's shoulders, which turn out to be the tips of thick ropes. Nimrod laughs as he handles each piece of rope and says:

Nimrod: These are the two serpents you scare people with? Put him inside the cave..

(points to the cave on one side of the stage)

Block the entrance and let him die inside.

Soldiers push Dahhak inside the cave and bring rocks to block the cave's entrance.

Nimrod *(to the crowd)*: I am the king now!

The crowd *(in amazement)*: What?! We only asked for your help!

Nimrod: Actually, I am your only lord!!

The crowd *(in amazement)*: What are you saying?

Nimrod *(addressing his soldiers)*: Bring them before me, one after the other..

Soldiers move forward, pushing the gathered people one by one. When the first person approaches, he squats down fearfully before Nimrod.

Nimrod: Who is your lord?

First person in the crowd: What?

Nimrod: Who is your lord?

First person in the crowd: I don't know!!

Nimrod kicks the first person in the crowd, he falls to the ground and then Nimrod picks up Dahhak's spear from the ground and stabs him.

He then puts his foot on the stabbed man's chest as he kicking and dying, and says:

Nimrod: Say Nimrod is my lord.. Bring the second one.

The second person in the crowd stands before Nimrod, and Nimrod asks:

Nimrod: Who is your lord?

The second person in the crowd: Nimrod

Nimrod then asks the third: Who is your lord?

The Third person in the crowd: Nimrod

Mixed voices: Who is your lord?

: Nimrod

: Who is your lord?

: Nimrod

: Who is your lord?

: Nimrod

and so on till the curtains close.

Act 2

Scene 1

The palace of Nimrod with his ministers and entourage.

Nimrod: They question my divinity.. And they say that there is a god in the heavens. There is no god but me. To prove to them that there is no other god, I raised four big eagles and trained them to eat meat. I then tied them to an open coffin in which I lay and raised a piece of meat with a stick which made the eagles fly high up.. I saw the ground below me and the heavens above me and I started searching for their claimed god. My hand got tired from raising the stick with the piece of meat, so it fell, and the meat fell down heading to the ground and the eagles followed the meat until they hit the ground, and still I never found their claimed god.

The minister: King.. You have dominated the whole world, east and west, there is no need to bother yourself with what they say. You are our lord, we all kneel before you.

All the entourage including the minister kneel before Nimrod and then return to their seats.

Nimrod: Minister.. Build a lofty tower for me, so that I can ascend to its top and make sure that there is no god except me, neither on earth nor in heaven.

The minister: Oh great lord.. The nation is hit by drought, the citizens are hungry and you have the food.. Give food to those who believe in you and those who do not shall be deprived. The people are gathered now before your gates.

Nimrod: Good idea. Let the people enter one by one.

The minister: Doorkeeper, let the people enter one by one.

The Minister stands as people enter to meet Nimrod, and upon receiving the first person of the crowd, he says:

The Minister *(addressing the first person)*: If you want food you should kneel down to

Nimrod's feet. If he asks you *(who is your lord?)* you should answer *(Nimrod is my lord)*.

The first of the people approaches Nimrod, and falls to his knees before him then straightens up while seated.

Nimrod: Who is your lord?

First person: Nimrod is my lord.

Nimrod: Give him food.

Second person approaches and the minister receives him, telling him the same as the one before, and he kneels before Nimrod then straightens up while seated.

Nimrod: Who is your lord?

Second applicant: Nimrod is my lord.

Nimrod: Give him food.

Third person of the poeple approaches, the minister receives him telling him the same as the one before, and again kneels before Nimrod then straightens up while seated.

Nimrod: Who is your lord?

Third applicant: Nimrod is my lord.

Herein the treasury official enters in a hurry, kneels down in prostration, then straightens up in a seated position, addressing Nimrod:

Treasury official: Oh great lord, thousands of people are gathered outside of the palace, and the food is not enough for all of them. How would we provide food for the armies?!

Construction expert: Oh great lord.. I am experienced in construction, I will build you a great tower from which you may reach the layers of the heavens.

As for the people, they can work in construction and be paid for their efforts. This will alleviate the famine.

Nimrod: That is right.. Good idea.. Go ahead construction expert, and we will provide you with the money for building the tower.. Let's call it the Tower of Babel.

Everyone is then ordered to facilitate the expert's mission.

Everyone: We have heard your command and we will obey Oh great lord.

Blackout

Scene 2

In front of the Tower of Babel.

The public is gathered awaiting Nimrod's arrival:

Nimrod arrives. He is received and welcomed by the construction expert.

Construction expert: Welcome, oh great lord.. The construction was completed as soon as possible. We have used burned brick, and made use of tar and bitumen to adhere the structure together. I will also show you oh great lord the way we made it.

The expert calls upon some of the workers to bring burnt brick and tar.

Construction expert: Workers, bring the bricks and the bitumen.

Workers bring some bricks and using the bitumen to stick them together.

The expert takes two bricks to Nimrod, fixes them together using the tar, suggests to Nimrod to try separating them and says:

Construction expert: Oh great lord, no power can detach these two bricks.

The expert then invites Nimrod to go inside the tower:

The expert: Come inside great lord, enter the tower and ascend to the top of the tower, where you can see the heavens for yourself.

Nimrod *(before heading to the inside of the tower)*: People, I am going to ascend to the heavens to prove to you that no there is no god but me, and if I found anyone claiming to be god, I will bring them to you and kill them before you.

As Nimrod heads toward the tower, a strong wind gusts and the whole place starts shaking.. Bricks fall down causing sounds of a great collapse and huge dust. The screams are getting louder. Workers and soldiers search under the rubble and find the dead body of the construction expert under a pile of brick. The entourage searches for Nimrod until they find him. His face covered with dust, they started to rid him from the dirt. Nimrod stands up and faces the public, he stumbles as he walks and drags his feet as he leaves the stage.

Blackout

Scene 3

Nimrod's palace and he is sitting with his entourage.

Nimrod: Neither the eagles could take me to heavens, nor the Tower of Babel could raise me up there. But I will fight the god on earth by provoking jibes and mockery between people against the god. I will unite the people through the Syriac language and write down all my fables in this language.

Herein enters the minister harrowingly and yelling:

The minister: Oh great lord.. A calamity has hit the nation!!

Nimrod: What do you mean? Speak.

The minister: The nation of Babel has been divided. After having only one spoken language, Syriac, the nation now speaks 72 languages.

Nimrod rises furiously and stands at the center of the stage:

Nimrod: What do you say? How should we address them?

Nimrod moves around the stage clapping his hands and shaking his head as he says:

Nimrod: Who will speak to whom? Who will speak to whom? Who will speak to whom? Who will speak to whom?

He continues as such until the curtain closes.

Act 3

Scene 1

The palace of Nimrod.

Nimrod on his throne, thinking.. And the minister enters:

The minister: Oh great lord.. The lands of Babel has broken into 72 groups, each calls for its independence. The kingdom will fall. You must do something.

Nimrod: What shall I do?!! We kill.. We get killed.

We torture.. We get tortured.

We throw people in jail.. We will be imprisoned.

A man dressed in white enters.. He's an angel that

only Nimrod can see and hear. The minister can neither see nor hear this man in white.

The angel: God tells you: Believe in me and I will let you keep your kingdom.

Nimrod: Is there a god other than me?!

The minister: Lord, what are you saying?!

Nimrod: Nothing.. Nothing.

The angel disappears and the treasury official enters.

Treasury official: Lord.. We are running short on money, and the armies are calling for allocations and threatening to reject uprising a war.. And if they reject uprising a war, the kingdom will collapse.

Nimrod: What should I do?!! I have used all means; plundering, looting and confiscating the people's money..

Herein enters the angel, not seen nor heard by the treasury official as well:

The angel: God tells you: Believe in me and I will let you keep your kingdom.

Nimrod: Is there a god other than me?!

The Treasury official: Lord, what are you saying?!

Nimrod: Nothing.. Nothing.

Herein enters the army commander:

The army commander: Oh lord.. The nation is turbulent.. You should take decisive measures or otherwise your rule will come to an end.

Nimrod: What shall I do? Give me advice.Everyone is consumed thinking..

Herein enters the angel, not seen nor heard by the army commander:

The angel: God tells you: Believe in me and I will let you keep your kingdom.

Nimrod: Is there a god other than me?

The minister, the treasury official and the army commander are in shock, and they do not know to whom Nimrod is speaking.

The angel: Gather your armies.. We meet tomorrow at sunset.

Then the angel vanishes.

Nimrod *(talking to himself)*: I will gather my armies.. And we meet tomorrow at sunset.

Nimrod *addressing the minister, the treasury official and the army commander*: I will gather my armies.. The encounter will be tomorrow.. Tomorrow at sunset.. Prepare yourselves, for the war will be tomorrow.. Tomorrow at sunset..

The minister, the treasury official and The army commander: Who are we going to war with?

Nimrod (as if having lost his mind and hallucinating):

Nimrod: I don't know. However the war is tomorrow. With whom?! I do not know!

Blackout

Scene 2

The palace of Nimrod..

Nimrod is sitting and two soldiers are looking from a porch at the army outside of the palace:

The first soldier: The army is fully assembled. Standing line after line! Some citizens are watching the army.

The second soldier: The sun has set and the enemy's army is nowhere to be seen!

The first soldier: Something is covering the sun.

The second soldier: It is a cloud.

The first soldier: It is approaching at a tremendous speed.

The second soldier: It is a mosquito cloud.

Both soldiers yell: The mosquitos are eating the soldiers flesh and drinking their blood. The soldiers are trying to resist and fight back.

Nimrod hurries up to the porch.

Nimrod: This is strange.. What am I seeing? The mosquitos are eating my soldiers and not harming the citizens.. What is this?! My army is being turned into skeletons?!

A mosquito cloud enters to where Nimrod is, so one of the soldiers hides behind the right side curtain and the other behind the left side curtain. Nimrod takes shelter at one of the pillars and starts hitting his head to the pillar.

A group of citizens (A) appear from around the right side of the stage curtain, they look about but see nothing. They then slowly enter the room, only to drag out the first soldier's skeleton to the center of the stage.. Upon seeing this occurrence they let out a loud cry:

One of the group of citizens (A) shouts:

The skeleton of Nimrod!!

A Group of citizens (B) appear from around the left side of the stage curtain, they look around and come

in dragging at their feet to the center of the stage a skeleton of the second soldier.. Upon seeing this, they let out a loud cry:

One of the group of citizens (B):

This is the skeleton of Nimrod!!

A person holding a soldier's ripped clothes approaches and says:

Person: These clothes belong to this skeleton.. He is one of the soldiers.

Then another person approaches holding a soldier's ripped clothes and says:

Another person: So these clothes belong to this skeleton.. He is also one of the soldiers.

One of the group of citizens (A) says:

Then, where is Nimrod?!

They start searching for him all around.. Until they find him still banging his head to the pillar.. They take him to the center of the stage.

One of the group of citizens (B):

The mosquitos haven't eaten you?!

One of the group of citizens (A):

So, you are a god!!

Nimrod: I am no god.. I wish the mosquitos had eaten me.. A mosquito made it through my nose and ended up in my brain. Hit me on the head until the mosquito is out.. Hit me on the head.. Oh my head, my head!!

Everyone from both groups start hitting Nimrod with both hands, one after the other.. And then they beat him with slippers. Some of them hit Nimrod on his neck.. But Nimrod points to his head and says:

Nimrod: Here.. Here.. The pain subsides when I am hit on the head.

Someone stands facing the audience beyond the stage, and shouts:

One of the group of citizens (A):

Let whoever wants to take revenge against Nimrod come!

Nimrod (crying): Beat me on the head.. Beat me on the head..

The number increases, each one holding a slipper, and beats Nimrod on his head.

The curtain closes as Nimrod says:

Nimrod: Hit me on the head..
Hit me on the head..
Hit me on the head..

End

www.ingramcontent.com/pod-product-compliance
Ingram Content Group UK Ltd.
Pitfield, Milton Keynes, MK11 3LW, UK
UKHW021958190726
13853UKWH00004B/1611

9 789948 360568